MMA
MIXED MARTIAL ARTS™

MUAY THAI BOXING

Greg Roza

WITH STEP-BY-STEP STOP-ACTION
MOVES BY *BEN DANIEL*

rosen publishing's
rosen
central®

New York

For Sensei Dawn Giancarlo—Sandan in Isshinryu Karate. "Happy birthday, Merry Christmas!" — Greg Roza

Dedicated to my loving Sensei, Master Mal Perkins, 6th Dan. This wouldn't have come to fruition without the love and training you have given me over the years. Hail, Master Mal! — Sensei Ben Daniel

Published in 2013 by The Rosen Publishing Group, Inc.
29 East 21st Street, New York, NY 10010

Copyright © 2013 by The Rosen Publishing Group, Inc.

Descriptions of moves by Sensei Ben Daniel and Sensei Mike Messina. "Chicken wing" move created by Ben Daniel.

First Edition

This book is published only as a means of providing information on unique aspects of the history and current practice of martial arts. Neither Rosen Publishing nor the author makes any representation, warranty, or guarantee that the techniques described or photographs included in this book will be safe or effective in any self-defense situation or otherwise. You may be injured if you apply or train in the techniques of self-defense presented in this book, and neither Rosen Publishing nor the author is responsible for any such injury that may result. It is essential that you consult a parent or guardian regarding whether or not to attempt any technique described in this book. Specific self-defense techniques shown in this book may not be called for in a specific set of circumstances or under applicable federal, state, or local law. Neither Rosen Publishing nor the author makes any representation or warranty regarding the legality or appropriateness of any technique mentioned in this book.

Library of Congress Cataloging-in-Publication Data

Roza, Greg.
Muay Thai boxing/Greg Roza.
    p. cm.—(MMA: mixed martial arts)
Includes bibliographical references and index.
ISBN 978-1-4488-6963-3 (library binding)
1. Muay Thai. I. Title.
GV1127.T45R69 2013
796.815—dc23

2011047959

Manufactured in the United States of America

CPSIA Compliance Information: Batch #S12YA: For further information, contact Rosen Publishing, New York, New York, at 1-800-237-9932.

CONTENTS

INTRODUCTION

A martial art is a system of exercises and traditions originally designed for use in hand-to-hand combat. Martial arts students practice techniques for years to become proficient in their application in real-life situations.

Dozens of martial arts—from aikido to wrestling—have been developed over the centuries. Long ago, ancient cultures all over the world created their own forms of martial arts for use in hunting and battle. Some feature weapons, from the bamboo sticks of escrima to the razor-sharp blades of kenjutsu.

A monk of the Shaolin Temple in Dengfeng, China, demonstrates the ancient art of Shaolin kung fu.

Some martial arts, such as Bruce Lee's jeet kune do, were developed within the past one hundred years. Yet, the many forms of kung fu—perhaps the oldest of all martial arts—took root in China more than four thousand years ago.

Primitive people first developed martial arts techniques while hunting wild animals. Soldiers used hunting as a way to train for battle. As armies grew and became more powerful, so, too, did their martial arts abilities. Spiritual men known as "warrior monks" refined certain techniques, creating more sophisticated versions of kung fu. Even peasants, looking for ways to defend themselves, their families, and their property, developed new kung fu styles, many of which used farm tools as weapons.

Over the centuries, generation after generation of kung fu students mastered the techniques of their ancestors, modified them, and developed new techniques. Two distinct methods arose, known as hard and soft techniques. The ancient methods slowly transformed and branched out into the many schools that exist today. Chinese kung fu influenced the development of martial arts in other countries, such as the many Japanese schools of karate, as well as the muay Thai style of Thailand.

Today, soldiers and law enforcement officials all over the world are trained in the martial arts. Many armies have even developed their own special martial art—such as krav maga of the Israeli Army. However, martial arts are no longer viewed as bloodthirsty methods of battle. They have been transformed into comprehensive systems used to maintain peace and safety.

Many "civilians" begin training in the martial arts to stay physically fit. Others, including many children, train to learn how to defend themselves. Most instructors will tell you, too, that the martial arts are an excellent way of learning discipline and respect, as well as improving one's mental and spiritual well-being.

The knowledge and practice of multiple martial arts is called mixed martial arts, or MMA. It's a growing sport in the United States and has been popular in other countries as well. The athletes who participate in MMA have diverse backgrounds, but they all have one thing in common: they have trained in two or more martial arts and use that knowledge during one-on-one competitions with others like them. Some of the most common martial arts used in MMA include karate, muay Thai, judo, and Brazilian jiu-jitsu.

There are several ways of winning an MMA match. A knockout, or KO, occurs when one of the opponents loses consciousness because of a strike.

Female featherweight muay Thai fighters say a ceremonial Buddhist prayer before the start of a match in Bangkok, Thailand.

A technical knockout, or TKO, occurs when the referee feels a fighter can no longer defend himself or herself from the opponent, or when a serious injury occurs. During a submission, a fighter admits defeat by signaling, usually by tapping, that he or she wants or needs to stop. This occurs most often because of submission holds, such as joint locks and choke holds. If the two fighters each make it through an entire fight, a group of judges decides which fighter wins based on points earned during the match.

Muay Thai, the official sport of Thailand, is no different from other martial arts discussed above. Its development is rooted in Thailand's rich history, originating thousands of years ago as a style of combat and a method of self-defense. Throughout the ages it has transformed into a cultural treasure.

Muay Thai has had a growing influence on other forms of martial arts. Many fighters in the sport of kickboxing train in muay Thai. More and more MMA fighters learn muay Thai and bring its special skills to competitions. It's an aggressive fighting style with numerous strikes, blocks, and holds designed to knock an opponent down quickly. In MMA fighting, the ability to strike quickly and forcefully can help swing the momentum in your favor. It can also put an end to the fight before your opponent sees it coming.

Muay Thai plays a specific role during an MMA competition. Fighters use its aggressive tactics to attack quickly and knock their opponent down. Once that occurs, a fighter may choose another style to finish the fight. For example, much of the fighting in MMA occurs "on the ground." That's when grappling and submission moves come into play. At that point, muay Thai skills take a backseat to styles like Brazilian jiu-jitsu.

The story of muay Thai is an interesting one. It has come a long way from an ancient fighting style to become a component of modern MMA.

CHAPTER 1

UNDERSTANDING MUAY THAI

In Thai, *muay* means "boxing," and the fighting style is often simply called Thai boxing. It's a "stand-up" fighting style based on quick strikes and skillful holds known as clinches.

In Thailand, muay Thai is not just a martial art. It's a system of cultural traditions passed down through the centuries. Muay Thai customs are an important part of the sport, as well as the Thai culture itself. Traditional music is played during matches, as it was hundreds of years ago. Before each bout, fighters perform a "dance" to traditional music to show respect to their teachers and gyms. The fighters wear traditional armbands and headbands.

In the past few decades, muay Thai has gained popularity around the world. It's widely considered one of the most effective hand-to-hand combat styles because of its devastating strikes. MMA fighters who combine muay Thai with ground fighting styles are often the most successful and exciting to watch.

WHAT IS MUAY THAI?

MMA fighters have a wide range of styles. Some, such as jiu-jitsu experts, take the fight to the ground where they apply holds and joint locks. Others, such as judo practitioners, use throws to beat their opponents. Muay Thai fighters, however, use hard, quick strikes to beat their opponents.

Unlike western boxing, which requires the use of fist attacks only, muay Thai offers a wider range of weapons. In addition to fists, muay Thai weapons include feet, elbows, and knees, providing a fighter with eight weapons in all. It's often referred to as the "science of eight limbs."

Muay Thai is a style that requires great skill and physical fitness. During a single fight, the audience sees spinning elbow strikes, high kicks, powerful jumps, and wrestling moves. The ancient form of muay Thai—known as muay boran, or ancient boxing—included more extravagant attacks that are seldom seen in modern muay Thai. These include head butts (the

Young muay Thai students participate in a traditional dance during the Wax Castle Festival in northeastern Thailand. This festival celebrates the end of the monsoon season.

THE RULES OF MUAY THAI

Originally, organized muay Thai competitions were far more dangerous. Injuries and even deaths occurred. Some reports even say that fighters sometimes wore hand wrappings dipped in glue and broken glass. As organized fighting grew in popularity, the rules were changed to protect fighters.

Basic equipment includes shorts, padded gloves, a mouth guard, and groin protection. Some divisions allow joint protection and headgear. Muay Thai tradition also allows colorful armbands and headbands.

Professional fights last for five, three-minute rounds with two-minute breaks in between. The competitors are matched based on weight, and each is weighed before the fight. Opponents may hit, kick, and push each other. They can use every part of their bodies except for their heads. Fighters may not strike their opponents in the eyes, back, or groin; doing so may result in a penalty or disqualification. Fights are decided by a knockout or by judges if both fighters are still standing after five rounds.

ninth weapon), and moves where the attacker literally climbs up his or her opponent's body, usually stepping off the front leg in order to land a deadly blow from above.

Also important to the style are holds, or clinches. A clinch brings both fighters tightly together where elbow and knee strikes can be devastating. Using the clinch well can help dictate the course of the fight. Falling victim to a strong clinch, or failing to clinch an opponent properly, can result in a quick knockout.

THE HISTORY AND EVOLUTION OF MUAY THAI

The ancient Thais were probably nomads from southwest China. Between the ninth and thirteenth centuries, the Thais slowly migrated into Southeast Asia. They fought with numerous groups during this time, including the Burmese and Khmer (Cambodian) civilizations. The ancient Thai fighting style was most likely influenced by these cultures.

The Thais developed a system of fighting that used swords, spears, and knives, as well as "empty handed" fighting techniques. This system, known as krabi krabong, is still practiced by some today. When Thai soldiers lost their weapons during combat, they were taught to defend themselves with their fists, elbows, knees, and feet. This was the origin of modern muay Thai.

In the thirteenth century, the Thais overthrew their Khmer rulers and founded a Thai kingdom. Hostilities between the cultures in Southeast Asia continued for the next four hundred years. During this time, the Thais refined the arts of krabi krabong and muay Thai. Muay Thai became tightly woven into the Thai culture. Kings and farmers alike practiced the martial art.

Female Islamic students practice the ancient art of krabi krabong at a private school in Saiburi, Thailand.

The Thai kingdom was annexed by Burma in 1569. In 1592, the Thai prince Narasuen defeated a Burmese prince in a duel and then forced the Burmese out of the area. Thai leaders continued to improve muay Thai. Regional styles were compared and merged to strengthen the martial art. The Thai king Pra Chao Sua, known as the Tiger King, enjoyed muay Thai so much

Two muay Thai boxers spar amid the ancient ruins of Ayuthaya, the original capital of the Thai kingdom.

that he frequently disguised himself to participate in, and win, local fighting competitions.

In 1767, the Burmese burned Ayuthaya—the center of the Thai kingdom—to the ground. Much of the written history of the Thai culture was lost. In 1770, the Burmese king asked captured Thais if anyone wanted to fight for his freedom. Stories say that a prisoner named Nai Kha Nom Tom defeated ten of Burma's greatest warriors to earn his freedom. Today, "Muay Thai Day" is celebrated on March 17 in his honor.

The Thai people soon recaptured their land. In 1782, leader Rama I became the first ruler of the Chakri dynasty, which is still in power today. Since that time, muay Thai has changed from a system of combat to a wildly popular sport. The fighting gear has improved and the more deadly attacks were outlawed to keep fighters safe. Modern Thai fighters continue to improve the sport while performing for millions of fans, in person and on television.

TRAINING FOR MUAY THAI

Continuous training has long been an important part of muay Thai. Hundreds of years ago, the Thais relied on the natural world for training. They used banana trees to practice kicking. They used coconuts floating in water to practice punching. Today, muay Thai training takes place in gyms with cutting-edge equipment.

New students spend most of their time learning the correct way to stand and move. After that, they begin practicing the many different kinds of attacks, and they drill them over and over. Even the most knowledgeable fighters practice repetitive kicks and punches to stay at the top of their game.

Muay Thai attacks range from straightforward punches and kicks to spinning elbows and leaping knee attacks. These advanced attacks require agility and flexibility. Because of this, fighters spend time stretching their muscles before training and before fights.

Women were once banned from muay Thai competitions. Today, however, female matches are gaining popularity all over Thailand and around the world.

Stamina is another important factor in muay Thai. Fighters are taught not to show weakness or fatigue, even when injured—revealing this only gives their opponent an edge. Training includes numerous stamina exercises, including shadow boxing, weight training, clinch training, sparring, and long hours of pad work.

MUAY THAI TODAY

Some people view MMA as a barbaric sport. But the truth is its athletes are some of the most skilled, fit, and respected in the world. In some countries, such as Japan, Thailand, and Brazil, MMA fighters are superstars, similar to professional football and basketball players in the United States. Thanks to MMA organizations such as the Ultimate Fighting Championship (UFC) and televised distribution through national networks such as Spike TV and FOX, the sport has gained momentum in the United States. Televised competitions have earned fans in this country who previously didn't know that MMA even existed. The increased application of muay Thai techniques in MMA fighting has brought the ancient art to a much wider audience than ever before.

CHAPTER 2

STARS OF MUAY THAI

Muay Thai practitioners strive to become masters of the "science of the eight limbs." They spend years in specialized training, learning to use chock (fist techniques), sok (elbow techniques), te (kicking techniques), and khow (knee techniques from a distance). They also train in clinch techniques, which they call garn goad plum tee khow. When combined into a single style, these techniques produce one of the most aggressive martial arts in the world. Muay Thai is a direct style of martial arts, with its foremost goal being to incapacitate an opponent with speed, power, and precision.

It's no surprise, then, that MMA fighters have discovered the benefits of muay Thai. As a training tool, muay Thai strengthens and conditions fighters, while helping them to increase their speed and accuracy at the same time. In battle, muay Thai is a dangerous weapon that can bring a fight to an end quickly.

Although the finest muay Thai fighters come from Thailand, the martial art has become popular in countries around the world. Many of the best MMA fighters are now using it with great success. Fighters from England, the United States, and the Netherlands have added muay Thai to their arsenal with great results. As you will see from the fighters highlighted in this chapter, however, many of the best muay Thai MMA fighters today are from Brazil.

SAENCHAI SINBIMUAYTHAI

Saenchai Sinbimuaythai, once known by the name Saenchai Sor Kingstar, is considered by many to be the greatest muay Thai fighter in the world today. Raised in northeast Thailand, Saenchai began training when he was just eight years old. Soon after that, people quickly took notice of the tough and talented youngster when he appeared in matches. When he was fourteen, Saenchi moved to Bangkok to train with veteran fighters. When he was just fifteen, he became the Lumpinee Stadium super flyweight champion.

Run by the Thai government, Lumpinee Stadium is considered the center of the muay Thai universe. To win a championship there at age fifteen was an incredible accomplishment.

As Saenchai matured, he continued to amaze fans with his technical style and exciting finishes. He defeated so many contenders that he started challenging fighters outside of his weight range. Saenchai won three more Lumpinee championships, one in the bantamweight, super featherweight, and lightweight divisions. At times he fought, and beat, competitors who were 20 pounds (9 kilograms) heavier than he was. Many experts like to say that, pound for pound, Saenchai is the best fighter in the history of muay Thai.

After such complete success in Thailand, Saenchai wanted to challenge himself. He began to travel and face fighters from other countries. He first traveled to the nearby countries of the Philippines and Japan. However, he has traveled as far as the Netherlands, the United Kingdom, and the United States. Everywhere he goes, Saenchai is the king of muay Thai.

In 2002, Saenchai decided to try western-style boxing. He fought in the Pan Asian Boxing Association (PABA). He won five out of five bouts and won the featherweight championship of that organization. Saenchai grew bored with western style boxing and returned to Thai boxing in 2004.

Saenchai continued to dominate his opponents in muay Thai in Thailand and around the world. He was the World Muay Thai Council (WMC) lightweight champion of 2010. He also won over many American fans by winning the Muay Thai Association of America (MTAA) lightweight championship of 2011. After more than fifteen years of championships, Saenchai still knows how to do it.

Like most muay Thai fighters, Saenchai is devoted to training. He stays in shape and constantly prepares for his next match. He attributes his longevity in muay Thai to developing a highly technical style that allows him to avoid injury while delivering punishing blows to his opponents. Over the years, Saenchai has fought outside Thailand more and more, ever in search of worthy opponents. One reason he likes doing this is because it gives him more freedom to perform unorthodox moves, such as his signature cartwheel kick. Few muay Thai athletes are good enough to pull off this highly difficult move.

In 2008, the Sport Authority of Thailand named Saenchai fighter of the year for the second time—he won the award first in 1999. This is a great accomplishment for a twenty-eight-year-old fighter. Now in his thirties, Saenchai plans to retire from professional muay Thai in the next few years. He wants to open his own gym and help train the muay Thai superstars of the future.

ANDERSON SILVA

Brazilian MMA fighter Anderson Silva is the current middleweight UFC champion. He holds the record for longest winning streak in UFC history with fourteen consecutive wins. Today, many experts and fans consider him the greatest fighter in MMA. This is in large part due to his impressive muay Thai skills.

Silva was born in 1975 and grew up in Curitiba, Brazil. When he was young, jiu-jitsu was very popular. However, his family was poor, and he could not afford lessons. Silva learned jiu-jitsu techniques by watching and sparring with people in his neighborhood. When he turned twelve, Silva's family enrolled him in tae kwon do lessons. He also trained in the Brazilian martial art of capoeira. At age sixteen, Silva moved on to muay Thai. In addition, he has since earned black belts in Brazilian jiu-jitsu, judo, and tae kwon do.

Silva did not have his first MMA fight until 2000, but he quickly rose to greatness thanks to his comprehensive training. In 2001, Silva went to Japan to fight in the Shooto MMA organization. Later that year, Silva beat the previously undefeated fighter Yahato Sakurai to win the Shooto middleweight championship. He then competed in the Pride Fighting Championships, which was at the time the biggest MMA organization in the world. Next, Silva competed in the Cage Rage Championships in the United Kingdom, for which he became the middleweight champion. In 2006, Silva came to the United States to fight in the UFC.

Silva's performance in the UFC has been outstanding. Few people in the United States knew of him, and he shocked fans by knocking out his first opponent, Chris Leben, in forty-five seconds. His next fight was against UFC middleweight champion Rich Franklin. Using a strong muay Thai clinch and a flurry of strikes, Silva defeated Franklin in three minutes and took over the title of middleweight champion. As of 2011, Silva has successfully defended his title nine times—a UFC record. He has yet to lose a UFC fight.

At 6 feet 2 inches (1.87 meters) tall, and with long arms and legs, Anderson "Spider" Silva's size has proved to be an asset in MMA. He is able to deliver punches and kicks while staying a safe distance from smaller opponents. Although Silva is comfortable fighting both on his feet and

On August 27, 2011, Anderson Silva *(right)* knocked out Yushin Okami in the second round of UFC 134 to defend his middleweight title.

on the ground, he is well known for his excellent muay Thai fighting style. Silva's muay Thai training has served him well. He is capable of delivering sudden and powerful fist and elbow strikes, which leave his opponents stunned and sometimes unconscious. In the clinch, Silva uses lightning-fast knee strikes to disable his opponents. If and when the fight ends up on the ground, Silva's Brazilian jiu-jitsu training allows him to end fights with submissions.

Anderson Silva always puts on a good show for fans. He has even successfully battled fighters in higher weigh divisions. Of his fourteen UFC wins, five have been knockouts, thanks mostly to his muay Thai training.

MAURICIO RUA

Mauricio "Shogun" Rua is an MMA fighter from Brazil. He currently fights in the UFC, and is a former light heavyweight champion in that organization. Rua was born on November 25, 1981, in Curitiba, Brazil. At the age of six, Rua began training in Brazilian jiu-jitsu. Just one year later, he began training in muay Thai. As Rua matured, he proved to be an accomplished fighter in jiu-jitsu and muay Thai competitions. Today, he has a black belt in Brazilian jiu-jitsu and is well known for his muay Thai techniques in the octagon.

Rua began fighting in martial arts competitions when he was sixteen years old. He was following in the footsteps of his older brother, Murilo. He did very well in Brazilian jiu-jitsu competitions, and quickly made a name for himself in Brazilian muay Thai by winning ten out of ten fights. In 2003, he became the middleweight champion of a Brazilian muay Thai organization.

In 2002, Rua began competing in MMA fighting. He quickly proved his abilities by winning four of his first five fights. Rua began fighting in Japan's Pride Fighting Championship organization in 2003. He continued to dominate the competition with his aggressive stand-up

On May 8, 2010, Mauricio Rua *(left)* knocked out Lyoto Machida in round 1 to become the UFC light heavyweight champion.

fighting style and became a star by defeating MMA greats such as Quinton Jackson and Ricardo Arona. In August 2005, Rua defeated Arona to become the Pride middleweight champion. With this victory, Rua became known as one of the best MMA fighters in the world.

In September 2007, Rua began his UFC career with a disappointing loss to Forrest Griffin. Fans noticed that the normally aggressive fighter didn't look prepared for the fight. However, Rua later revealed that he had injured his knee in practice. After several surgeries, Rua returned to the UFC with a victory against Mark Coleman. He looked even more like his old self in his next fight against former UFC light heavyweight champion Chuck Liddell.

Rua's next fight was against then-current lightweight champion Lyoto Machida. After five full rounds without a knockout, the judges ruled that Machida had won. However, many fans and experts felt Rua had been the better fighter. A rematch was held several months later. Rua came out strong and knocked Machita out in the first round to become the UFC light heavyweight champion.

"Shogun" Rua is an aggressive fighter. As in muay Thai competitions, Rua likes to use stand-up fighting with powerful punches and kicks. He likes to use sudden high kicks and flying knees to attack his opponents quickly. He's also a very good clinch fighter, using his knees to attack the head and body of his opponents. Once his opponents fall to the mat, Rua is well known for performing stomps and leaping strikes to knock them out.

WANDERLEI SILVA

Brazilian fighter Wanderlei Silva is a veteran MMA fighter with numerous victories. He's faced and beaten some of the greatest fighters in MMA, including Dan Henderson and Quinton "Rampage" Jackson.

Like Anderson Silva and Mauricio Rua, Wanderlei Silva is also from Curitiba, Brazil. He

In Thailand, many boys and young men train in muay Thai. It's a sign of pride and importance within the local community. However, muay Thai isn't closed to girls. In fact, the Thais considered it one of the best forms of physical fitness for all people, regardless of sex, age, or social class. Professional matches between women are a growing sport in Thailand and around the world.

Gina Carano is perhaps the best known female MMA fighter in the United States. Before her career in MMA, Carano trained and competed in muay Thai. She originally started training in the martial art to get in shape, but she found she was a natural at it. Carano has won twelve out of fourteen muay Thai matches.

Carano moved into MMA in 2006, when she was asked to fight in the first-ever sanctioned female MMA bout in Las Vegas, Nevada. Her muay Thai background has helped her to seven wins and just one loss in MMA. Even though she has improved her groundwork over the years, Carano is still known as a stand-up fighter with lightning-fast reflexes and punishing attacks.

was born in 1973 and began training in muay Thai when he was thirteen. Silva joined the military, where his talents as a fighter became noticeable. He soon joined the Brazilian vale tudo fighting organization, where there were very few rules and contestants fought without protective gloves. Silva dominated his opponents with non-stop punches and kicks. He earned the nickname Cachorro Louco ("Mad Dog") for his forceful and unrelenting fighting style.

Wanderlei Silva celebrates after a victory during UFC 139 in 2011.

Silva appeared in several UFC fights before joining the Japanese Pride Fighting Championship in its early years. He became one of the organization's best and most well-known fighters. Out of twenty-eight Pride matches between 1999 and 2007, Silva won an astounding twenty-two matches. Many of these wins resulted from knockouts. During this time period, Silva won an International Vale Tudo light heavyweight championship, and he was the Pride middleweight champion from 2001 to 2007.

In the UFC, Silva's record has been less spectacular. The closest he came to a championship was in April 2000, when he went a full five rounds with UFC great Tito Ortiz, only to lose by judges' decision. However, at thirty-seven years of age, Silva is still competing in the UFC and is still considered a true threat.

Silva's muay Thai experience has helped him become one of the greatest MMA fighters of all time. He attacks quickly with powerful punches and kicks. His greatest muay Thai weapon, however, is his masterful use of the clinch. Opponents who become trapped in Silva's clinch are subjected to repeated knee strikes to the head and body. Those who are unlucky enough to fall to the mat must guard themselves against Silva's devastating foot stomps.

CHAPTER 3

MUAY THAI STEP-BY-STEP

"I fear not the man who has practiced 10,000 kicks once, but I fear the man who had practiced one kick 10,000 times."

— *Bruce Lee*

Professional muay Thai fighters spend many years preparing for their fighting careers. They begin training around eight years of age, and continue throughout their twenties and thirties. Most professional muay Thai fighters retire at around thirty, although some make it to thirty-five. These fighters spend a quarter of their lifetime perfecting the martial art of their ancestors. Their efforts are apparent when the fight begins.

However, most muay Thai practitioners and trainers will tell you that it's never too late to train in the martial art. Learning the basic stances and attacks is a good way to get in shape. The training requires dedication and repetitive exercise, and it's a great way to stay fit. Men, women, and children around the world are using it for this purpose.

In this section, we will break down several of the essential muay Thai moves to get a better look at what it takes to perform them. Most of these moves can be practiced alone, with a punching bag, or with a partner. The best way to learn muay Thai or any other martial art, it should be noted, is with a trained professional. Muay Thai gyms are becoming more popular in the United States and chances are you can find one near where you live.

Remember to be safe while training. Some of these skills might be too hard for beginners. Also, the methods depicted in this book aren't meant to be used to attack others. Like any martial art, muay Thai is best used as a form of self-defense and for health reasons. Never use these skills to hurt other people.

JAB

Starting from the fighting stance, raise both hands to chin with elbows tucked (to protect from body blows). Tighten both fists with thumbs facing chin. Thumbs should touch middle fingers.

Bring front foot forward 3 inches (7.62 cm) and stand on ball of foot.

Turn front fist midway through the move with slight bend in elbow. Line up knuckle of index finger with nose.

Distribute 15 percent of weight on back foot and 85 percent on front foot, and then strike.

JAB TO CROSS COMBO

Perform jab as previously shown.

Following jab, pivot on ball of right foot, rotating left so that both hips are facing opponent. Position toes straight forward.

LEFT HOOK

Start from a fighting stance. With slight pressure on balls of both feet, drop left shoulder 1 inch (2.54 cm).

Generate momentum by rotating hips clockwise. Pivot left foot inward and point toes and knees right.

As you strike, turn right fist midway with a slight bend in the elbow and knuckle of index finger lining up with nose.

Exhale and pivot arm in a semicircular motion with knuckles facing right. At 80 percent completion of the strike, hook wrist inward.

Starting from the fighting stance, raise both hands to chin with elbows tucked (to protect from body blows). Tighten both fists with thumbs facing chin. Thumbs should touch middle fingers.

Drive off left foot and raise right knee to belly button, striking midsection.

UPPERCUT

Starting from the fighting stance, begin turning counterclockwise.

Slightly bend and begin to dip right knee while squaring hips to center.

REAR LEG FRONT KICK

Starting from the fighting stance, shift weight to rear foot.

Press off front foot to create momentum and bring right knee to hip height (chambering).

Dip right shoulder and lead fist through to strike the
face in an upward motion.

Extend leg at knee and strike with ball of foot, curling toes back
and away from opponent.

From the fighting stance, pivot front foot on heel so that toes are pointing left.

Rotate hips counterclockwise.

Chamber as right knee faces left
around hip height.

Extend knee and strike with top of
foot (instep) with toes pointing away
from opponent.

STEP BEHIND SIDE KICK

Start from a side stance—feet parallel and shoulder-width apart.

Move toward opponent by taking a baby step with left foot, then stepping with right foot behind left foot.

Driving off the right foot, chamber left knee up and bring left heel down.

ELBOW

Start in the fighting stance. With slight pressure on balls of both feet, drop left shoulder 1 inch (2.54 cm).

Extend left leg at the knee, striking with heel of foot while curling toes away from opponent.

Exhale and begin to strike with elbow in a semi-circular motion while rotating hips clockwise.

Strike opponent with forearm.

CHICKEN WING

From the fighting stance, begin to rotate hips clockwise and drop left hand to right hip.

Pivot off ball of left foot toward opponent.

Draw left fist from right hip across chest, extending and raising arm at an angle from shoulder height.

GLOSSARY

annex To add territory to a larger country.

arsenal A supply of weapons.

capoeira A combination martial art and dance form that originated in Brazil.

chamber To place an arm or leg in a position where it is prepared to attack or defend.

clinch In muay Thai, the act of grasping opponents tightly around the back of the neck and drawing them closer.

counterattack An attack made in response to an opponent's attack.

dominate To control completely.

dynasty A succession of rulers from the same family.

escrima A Filipino martial art that focuses on the use of bamboo sticks.

grapple To struggle with an opponent in close, hand-to-hand combat.

incapacitate To make someone unable to continue.

jeet kune do A martial art that is a mixture of several martial arts, created by Bruce Lee.

joint lock A grappling move that involves forcing a joint to bend or twist farther than it can naturally move, causing pain.

kenjutsu A Japanese martial art that means "the art of the sword."

krav maga An Israeli martial art known for its close combat skills and counterattacks.

migrate To move to a new area.

nomad Someone who travels instead of settling down.

octagon The area where UFC fights are held, which is a mat surrounded by an eight-sided fence.

practitioner Someone who participates in an activity or profession.

sanction To officially approve.

spar To practice fighting.

submission The act of withdrawing from a martial arts match due to pain.

tae kwon do A Korean martial art known for its extensive use of kicks.

unorthodox Failing to follow tradition.

veteran Someone who has a considerable amount of experience at something.

FOR MORE INFORMATION

Canadian National Martial Arts Association
1-3946 Quadra Street
Victoria, BC V8X 1J6
Canada
Web site: http://www.cnmaa.com
This organization seeks to unify martial arts athletes and communities across Canada.

International Brazilian Jiu-Jitsu Federation
Av Comandante Júlio de Moura 276
Barra da Tijuca
Rio de Janeiro, RJ 22620-012
Brazil
Web site: http://www.ibjjf.org
This federation was created by Carlos Gracie Jr. to represent the sport of Brazilian jiu-jitsu around the world.

Judo Canada

212 – 1725 St. Laurent
Ottawa, ON K1G 3V4
Canada
Web site: http://www.judocanada.org
Judo Canada is the national governing body for the art
of judo in Canada.

Thai Boxing Association of the U.S.A.

P.O. Box 4585
Carson, CA 90749
(724) 941-4900
Web site: http://www.thaiboxing.com
This is the oldest and largest muay Thai organization in
the United States, founded in 1968 by Ajarn Surachai
Sirisute.

U.S. Martial Arts Association

8011 Mariposa Avenue
Citrus Heights, CA 95610
(916) 727-1486
Web site: http://www.mararts.org
The U.S. Martial Arts Association aims to unify all
American martial arts.

World Amateur Muay Thai Association of Canada

164 Macatee Road
Cambridge, ON N1R 6Z8
Canada
Web site: http://www.wamtac.org
The World Amateur Muay Thai Association of Canada
is the governing and sanctioning body for amateur muay
Thai in Canada.

WEB SITES

Due to the changing nature of Internet links,
Rosen Publishing has developed an online list
of Web sites related to the subject of this book.
This site is updated regularly. Please use this link
to access the list:

http://www.rosenlinks.com/mma/muay

FOR FURTHER READING

Boraas, Tracey. *Thailand*. Mankato, MN: Capstone, 2006.

Delp, Christoph. *Muay Thai: Advanced Thai Kickboxing Techniques*. Berkeley, CA: North Atlantic Books, 2004.

Delp, Christoph. *Muay Thai Basics: Introductory Thai Boxing Techniques*. Berkeley, CA: Blue Snake Books, 2005.

Donovan, Sandra. *Teens in Thailand*. Minneapolis, MN: Compass Point Books, 2009.

Friedman, Mel. *Thailand*. New York, NY: Children's Press, 2009.

Haney, Johannah. *Capoeira*. New York, NY: Marshall Cavendish Benchmark, 2012.

Haney-Withrow, Anna. *Tae Kwon Do*. New York, NY: Marshall Cavendish Benchmark, 2012.

Harvey, Joe E. *Mastering Muay Thai Kick-Boxing: MMA Proven Techniques*. North Clarendon, VT: Tuttle Publishing, 2009.

Krauss, Erich, and Glen Cordoza. *Muay Thai Unleashed: Learn Technique and Strategy from Thailand's Warrior Elite*. New York, NY: McGraw-Hill, 2006.

Mack, Gail. *Kickboxing*. New York, NY: Marshall Cavendish Benchmark, 2012.

Rielly, Robin L. *Karate for Kids*. North Clarendon, VT: Tuttle Publishing, 2004.

Scandiffio, Laura. *The Martial Arts Book*. Toronto, ON, Canada: Annick Press, 2010.

Silva, Anderson, and Glen Cordoza. *MMA Instruction Manual*. Auberry, CA: Victory Belt Publishing, 2011.

Snowden, Jonathan, and Kendall Shields. *The MMA Encyclopedia*. Toronto, ON, Canada: ECW Press, 2010.

Villalobos, Pedro Solana, and Mark Van Schuyver. *Fighting Strategies of Muay Thai: Secrets of Thailand's Boxing Camps*. Boulder, CO: Paladin Press, 2002.

Wiseman, Blaine. *Ultimate Fighting*. New York, NY: Weigl Publishers, 2011.

Wouk, Henry. *Kung Fu*. New York, NY: Marshall Cavendish Benchmark, 2010.

BIBLIOGRAPHY

AskMen.com. "Anderson Silva." Retrieved August 8, 2011 (http://www.askmen.com/celebs/men/sports_60/94_anderson_silva.html).

Delp, Christoph. *Muay Thai Basics: Introductory Thai Boxing Techniques*. Berkeley, CA: Blue Snake Books, 2005.

Gina-Carano.org. "Gina Carano Biography." Retrieved August 8, 2011 (http://www.gina-carano.org/gina-carano-biography).

Goyder, James. "Saenchai Sor Kingstar: Interview with Muay Thai's Pound for Pound King." AsianCorrespondent.com, April 9, 2011. Retrieved August 8, 2011 (http://asiancorrespondent.com/52117/saenchai-sor-kingstar-interview-with-muay-thais-pound-for-pound-king).

Goyder, James, and Atchaa Khamlo. "Saenchai Sor Kingstar." *Muay Thai Phuket Magazine*, Issue 3. Retrieved August 8, 2011 (http://www.jamesgoyder.com/muaythai/issue_three.pdf).

History of Nations. "History of Thailand." Retrieved July 10, 2011 (http://www.historyofnations.net/asia/thailand.html).

Horizon Muay Thai Boxing Camp. "The History of Muay Thai Boxing." Retrieved July 10, 2011 (http://www.horizonmuaythai.com/history.html).

Iole, Kevin. "'Shogun' Has No One to Blame but Himself." Yahoo! Sports, October 5, 2009. Retrieved August 8, 2011 (http://uk.eurosport. yahoo.com/25102009/58/shogun-blame-him-self.html).

Krauss, Erich, and Glen Cordoza. *Muay Thai Unleashed: Learn Technique and Strategy from Thailand's Warrior Elite*. New York, NY: McGraw-Hill, 2006.

LeNg, Mike. "Saenchai Talks to the Science." The Science of 8 Limbs (blog). Retrieved August 8, 2011 (http://thescienceof8limbs. com/2010/12/20/saenchai-talks-to-the-science).

Lonely Planet. "Thailand History." Retrieved July 10, 2011 (http://www.lonelyplanet.com/ thailand/history).

Muay Thai Techniques. "An Idiot's Guide to Muay Thai Equipment and Muay Thai Gear." March 26, 2010. Retrieved July 12, 2011 (http://www. muaythaitechniques.org/muay-thai-techniques/ an-idiot%E2%80%99s-guide-to-muay-thai-equipment-and-muay-thai-gear).

Muay Thai Techniques. "Muay Thai in Mixed Martial Arts." March 14, 2010. Retrieved July 12, 2011 (http://www.muaythaitechniques. org/muay-thai-techniques/muay-thai-in-mixed-martial-arts).

Rousseau, Robert. "Anderson Silva." ExtremeProSports.com. Retrieved August 8, 2011 (http://www.extremeprosports.com/ MMA/anderson_silva.html).

Rousseau, Robert. "Biography and Profile of Mauricio 'Shogun' Rua." About.com. Retrieved August 8, 2011 (http://martialarts.about.com/ od/mmaandufc/p/shogunrua.htm).

Rousseau, Robert. "Biography and Profile of Wanderlei Silva." About.com. Retrieved August 8, 2011 (http://martialarts.about.com/od/ mmaandufc/p/wandsilva.htm).

Rousseau, Robert. "A History and Style Guide of Kung Fu." About.com. Retrieved July 1, 2011 (http://martialarts.about.com/od/styles/a/kungfu.htm).

Spider Silva's Fan Site. "Biography." Retrieved August 8, 2011 (http://madeira.hccanet.org/project1/cassidyp1/biography.html).

TalkKungFu. "History of Kung Fu." Retrieved July 1, 2011 (http://www.talkkungfu.co.uk/guides/history_of_kung_fu.html).

Villalobos, Pedro Solana, and Mark Van Schuyver. *Fighting Strategies of Muay Thai: Secrets of Thailand's Boxing Camps*. Boulder, CO: Paladin Press, 2002.

West, David. "The Axe Murderer." *Fighting Spirit Magazine*. Retrieved August 8, 2011 (http://www.fightingspiritmagazine.co.uk/article.asp?IntID=78).

INDEX

ABOUT THE AUTHOR

Greg Roza has been writing and editing educational materials for twelve years. He has a master's degree from SUNY Fredonia and lives in Hamburg, New York, with his wife and three kids. He recently earned his purple belt in isshin-ryu karate and is a white belt in Brazilian jiu-jitsu. Roza and his children are all on the road to becoming karate black belts.

ABOUT BEN DANIEL

Ben Daniel was born in Israel and raised in Margate, New Jersey. He has a bachelor of science degree in biology from Richard Stockton College of New Jersey. He has been training under Master Mal Perkins in American tae kwon do since age six and has also practiced Brazilian jiu-jitsu and hapkido each for nine years. Since receiving his first-degree black belt at sixteen, he has been teaching martial arts to students of all ages. He is now a third-degree black belt and is in training for his fourth-degree master's belt. He resides in New York, where he works as a professional personal trainer.

PHOTO CREDITS

Cover, pp. 1, 19, 24 © AP Images; p. 4 Cancan Chu/Getty Images; pp. 6, 11 Paula Bronstein/Getty Images; p. 9 Andrew Watson/Photolibrary/Getty Images; p. 12 Patrick Aventurier/Gamma-Rapho/Getty Images; p. 14 Pornchai Kittiwongsakul/AFP/Getty Images; p. 21 Richard Wolowicz/Getty Images.

Cover (inset images), pp. 8, 15, 25, and all photos on pages 26–39 by Cindy Reiman, assisted by Karen Huang.

Designer: Brian Garvey; Editor: Nicholas Croce; Photo Researcher: Cindy Reiman